£2
3/12

C000043604

Faces of humph

Caricatures and Memories

HUMPHREY LYTTELTON

Compiled and edited by Stephen Lyttelton

JR
BOOKS

First published in Great Britain in 2009 by
JR Books, 10 Greenland Street, London NW1 0ND
www.jrbooks.com

A catalogue record for this book is available from the British Library.

ISBN 978-1-906779-62-7

1 3 5 7 9 10 8 6 4 2

Printed by MPG Books, Bodmin, Cornwall

Acknowledgements

I would like to thank the following people for their help and assistance in putting this book together.

Alan Barnes, Susan Da Costa, Adrian Macintosh, Henrietta Lyttelton, Charlie and Lucy Lyttelton, Patricia Woods, Cath Strange, Elkie Brooks, Jon Naismith, Jim Simpson, Mary Stewart-Cox, Dave Bennett, Nick Hiley of the British Cartoon Archive, Jimmy Hastings, Steve Voce, and Lesley Wilson and Jessica Feehan at JR Books.

Foreword

Coming from a formal educational and social background, it is unsurprising that there was an expectation that Humphrey Lyttelton, my father, would follow in the footsteps of his forebears and of his father, an Eton Housemaster of great renown, into a scholastic career. Having at first elected to bow to tradition and become a schoolmaster himself, dad sent off for the university geography prospectus. It was not long – and hardly surprising! – that his tutors quickly realised that perhaps he was not cut out to follow this path. As he recalled:

> I became uneasy about the future, and uneasiness turned to horror as the prospectus for the geography diploma arrived from London University. It ran into several pages and appeared to cover every single material of the creation from astronomy to a detailed examination of the earth's crust. I had two years in which to take the diploma. It seemed to me that twenty was a more reasonable proposition, and even then I doubt I would have acquired more than a nodding acquaintance with the earth's crust.

It was with some trepidation that dad went to visit his father at Eton to express his doubts:

> After a certain amount of vague talk I took a deep breath and said tentatively: 'Sometimes I wonder whether I shall ever make it'.
> He was plainly relived that I had broached the subject.
> 'That', he said 'is a thought which has occurred to me too'.

It may be surprising to learn that throughout these early years the trumpet and a career in jazz played little part in my father's plans or daydreams. To him, it remained nothing more than a hobby, even though some paid gigs had been undertaken. To even contemplate abandoning the security blanket that his family, education and upbringing provided, for the world of jazz, was, at that stage, a step too far.

So dad decided, with his father's blessing, to embark on a career in illustration and he enrolled at the Camberwell School of Arts. At Camberwell his main interest was illustration: *John Minton and Susan Einzig had the most influence over me as a cartoonist – they were also contemporary figures who visited us in our habitat – the London jazz clubs.* Other classes such as architecture and the history of art were missed as he played truant or was hideously late. At times he had to resort to bribing the doorman, who would sign students in and out, with cigarettes so as not to be marked absent too often.

My father's cartoon career came about through his friendship with the clarinetist, Wally Fawkes, who worked at the *Daily Mail* as a cartoonist doing column breaks under the name of 'Trog'. Wally had been with the *Mail* for a while when Trog became a full size strip cartoon. Dad recalls how Wally got on the phone *'and tipped me the wink that the job of column breaker would soon be vacant'.* Searching for a pen name that would fit into the small cartoons, he came up with 'Humph', a pseudonym that was to be adopted in every area of his career. While at the *Mail* his cartoons would develop a style and humour of their own.

Dad's love of drawing never left him, even when he had moved on from the *Daily Mail* and become a full-time musician. It would always play a part in professional and family life: album sleeves, jazz club newsletters, programs and articles would all get the 'humph' treatment. Even his signature developed to include a caricature of himself playing trumpet with a speech bubble where he would put the message. Inevitably this would mean that he would spend sometimes hours after a concert signing autographs. Not that he would complain. Once, when on tour, returning from a gig up North, he stopped at a phone box to call home. As he waited for the call to connect he opened the phone directory hoping for some virgin pages which he could adorn with his doodles. Much to his delight and surprise he discovered the pages already covered with doodles from a previous visit some years before!

To Fred
with many
thanks —
I'm beginning
to enjoy being
doctored!
Humphrey
Lyttelton

At home you could not escape his drawings, as every blank piece of paper would be festooned with random caricatures. In assembling the material for this volume I went through every book in the house looking at the front and back inside covers for doodles. They were everywhere. The word 'doodle' doesn't, in fact, do justice to what I found. For a long time all our family Christmas cards were meticulously put together depicting various stages of family life, dogs and all. Many friends and family own humorous caricatures drawn for them, often sketched on the back of a beer mat or a napkin.

In this volume, I've tried to include a typical cross-section of his work, including many pictures kindly donated by those who knew him. I also buried myself in the diaries that dad left behind, written in his own meticulous calligraphic hand, as well as the many other pieces of writing from over the years. For as well as being a compulsive caricaturist he was, of course, also a prolific recorder of his own life. Where possible, therefore, I've tried to match his words with his pictures.

My research into the work dad did at the *Daily Mail* took me to two remarkable places: the British Cartoon Archive, housed in Kent University and The British Library Reading Room in Collindale. Not only did I find hitherto unseen cartoons but also some context to them and the era in which they were drawn.

I am not sure what I wanted when I first set out to put this book together. Many people had commented on the cartoons we had included in *Last Chorus* and had asked to see more and I hope they will be happy with the result. More importantly I hope this confection will raise a smile – that, after all, is what dad would have wanted.

Stephen Lyttelton

Faces of humph

Humph drew this unlikely caricature of himself while on holiday in Italy with his first wife, Patricia. It is, in fact, a very true likeness of him at this time.

I remember doing a gig at Southampton when I was with the George Webb Band around 1947. We had the jazz critic and writer Max Jones with us on the trip. Max was a diffident man, with a tendency to worry.

George, in common with many small men, has an abrupt, no-nonsense manner. When we got to the hall, a bit late, we didn't know how to get in. Max asked anxiously, 'Where's the front?' In his most assertive Cockney, George said, 'Round the back.'

One day Humph was just doing doodles of the band as women. The similarity of mine to Margaret Thatcher was completely coincidental! I was depping with the band a few years ago and had turned up with the wrong coloured clothing, so that I stuck out on stage like a blind cobbler's left thumb. I went to Humph's dressing room and told him. He turned a mock world-weary expression to me and said, 'I'm 80 years old – I don't give a fuck what trousers you wear!' Quite.

Alan Barnes, clarinet and alto sax
in Humph's band from 1988 to '93

Humph started his brief cartoon career at the *Daily Mail*, drawing what were then called 'column breakers' – small humorous cartoons that 'livened' up the letters page of the 'Mailbag'. He was soon in demand from feature editors and columnists alike, and the cartoons began to have an identity of their own, becoming known as 'Humphs'. Thus was spawned the pseudonym that stuck with him for his entire career.

"Et comment va Mister 'Iggins ce soir?"

The label was founded in 1983. It was not the first time that Humph had started his own label. In 1948/49 he felt the urge to be independent and launched London Jazz. The result was five 78rpm records, each one a (very) limited edition for distribution to fans of the band. So how come another dash for independence and the founding of Humph's Calligraph label thirty-five years later? The recording industry has become a monster, prompting many artists to break away from high-pressure intermediaries and embrace the principle that 'small' is best. So, for the first vinyl album on Calligraph that came out in 1984, Humph chose the studio, the photographer and the printers himself and brought in a guest, Wally Fawkes, his old friend and colleague from the early band. The choice was symbolic as it was Wally who, in the private studio in which we made our DIY London Jazz recording, lobbed a still-smouldering cigarette end in to a bin of inflammable waste-product and brought the session to end in a cloud of impenetrable smoke.

Introducing CALLIGRAPH RECORDS.....

"... it seems like yesterday!"

HUMPHREY LYTTELTON
Bruce Turner Pete Strange John Barnes
Paul Bridge Mick Pyne Adrian Macintosh
and Wally Fawkes

Available in all record shops through P.R.T., or by mail order. For signed copies, send to :- Calligraph Records, P.O. Box 60, Barnet, Herts, EN5 3LR, enclosing cheque or postal order for £6 incl. of post & package.

HUMPHREY LYTTELTON & HIS BAND
with their guest, WALLY FAWKES

"... it seems like yesterday!"

Calligraph Records

CLG LP 01

My band toured alongside Eddie Condon's when they came over after the Musician's Union ban had been lifted in the late 1950s. One day we stopped at a little pub in the West Country for lunch. Having had a double Scotch for his 'breakfast', Eddie pushed his hat on the back of his head, strolled over to some local rustics, stared and then asked, 'Are you guys poachers?'

HUMPHREY LYTTELTON and RUSSELL DAVIES present…

Gonna call my children home

THE WORLD OF

BUDDY BOLDEN

Starring

HUMPHREY LYTTELTON
as BUDDY BOLDEN

and RUSSELL DAVIES JOHN BARNES RANDY COLVILLE
ALAN ELSDON HENRY LOWTHER PETE STRANGE JIM BRAY
KEITH GRAVILLE COLIN BOWDEN RON WEATHERBURN

Did the Buddy Bolden session this evening. I got everyone to the Maida Vale studio at 6 o'clock for rehearsal. Yesterday I wrote out the themes we are going to play with the exact phrasing that I shall use, so that we shall get the correct, unison, ensemble sound. By 7.30, when we started recording, we had a good, authentic sound. Everyone was elated by the session and not only because both Russell D. and David Perry produced bottles of Scotch.

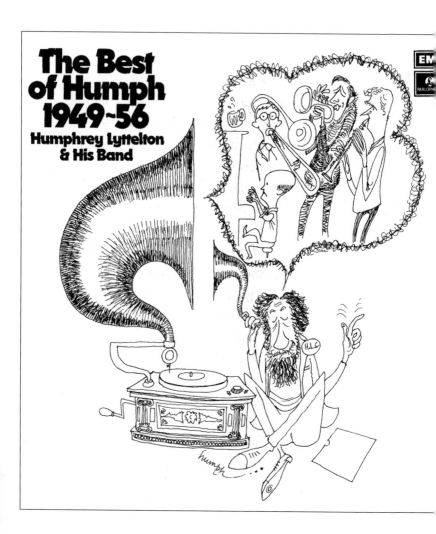

This is a sleeve done for a retrospective album. Humph liked to have talented young musicians in his band. He did this to keep the band fresh and, as he would regularly announce at live concerts, it would significantly lower the average age of the band!

However, throughout our childhood, he was far less tolerant of the music we would listen to:

One hears it said nowadays that contemporary 'beat' music, emerging as it does directly from teenage activity, has brought music closer to real life than it has been for half a century. To test this thesis, we have only to cast an ear over the so-called 'Liverpool sound' and ask ourselves how much, in fact, it tells us about Liverpool in 1964.

Listen to the Beatles 'Just Seventeen' – is this really the way Liverpool youth talks today? 'way beyond compare', 'dance with another'? They sound more in keeping with throaty tenors in a late Victorian drawing room.

This *Daily Mail* cartoon from 1950 conjures up many happy memories of our childhood holidays. Dad's sandcastles were always spectacular and never subscribed to tradition; we would stand proudly on Harlech beach as passers-by stopped to admire the life-size crocodiles and dragons. Then of course there were the holes – huge pits dug for no real reason other than he could!

Saturday 1st January 1977

*F*irst entry in this new, jumbo-sized diary. Collected the cash for last night and drove off. Pouring rain to start with, but a few miles down the road I began to notice cars coming in the opposite direction with thick masks of snow. Soon ran into what amounted to a blizzard, closing the 'fast lane' of the M6 and reducing speed to 20–30 mph. In the evening, watched a rather touching little TV film called 'Love among the Ruins' with Katherine Hepburn and Lawrence Olivier. One notices, especially in the midst of Christmas fare of TV, when something literate is offered.

Monday 3rd December 1979, Jeddah

One of the sights pointed out to us on the journey to Yarmouk was what remains of the Roman city of Jerash. On the way back, we call on our Jordanian driver to pull off the road at the spot and we spill out and clamber down to a wide Roman street lined with an avenue of pillars. It's a mad and magical feeling to stroll at midnight into the huge forum and sit around on the remains. After a while I hear the furious barking of a dog somewhere in the hills and getting rapidly nearer. With rabies in mind, it seems a good idea to re-embark. Halfway up the track leading to the road, I look up and, in a vivid, heart-thumping moment of fantasy, see the figure of Christ, bearded and robed, silhouetted against the light sky. It's our driver, who has got impatient and has walked out on to a promontory to see where we have got to.

—you'll find no lack of pudding-bowl hair-cuts in the jazz clubs

There's a tendency to type-cast the jazz fraternity as a sort of watered-down version of America's Beat Generation – tousled, be-jeaned, and relaxed almost to the point of total collapse. Of course, these types exist – you'll find no lack of pudding-bowl hair-cuts and grubby bare feet in the jazz clubs, whether it be in London's Soho, the Paris Left Bank, the hillside caves of Zurich or the 'New Orleans Clubs' of Hamburg or Dusseldorf. But because they most readily catch the eye, it is a mistake to think that they ARE the jazz world.

This 1949 drawing (more than a cartoon) accompanied an article that described the life of a Black labourer from Georgia. It was a time when the overt violence was dwindling (only two lynchings that year) but the general rule remained amongst the whites – 'You've gotta keep those Negroes down'.

There is an old man of Hatch End
Old watches and clocks he will mend.
He paints them bright red
Then he takes them to bed
It's driving his wife round the bend.

Some people think that Edward Lear invented the limerick for his Book of Nonsense in 1846. (Make the most of this scholarship – it's all you're going to get.) Wrong again! He wasn't even very good at it, running out of steam – and rhyme – by line five and going back rather feebly to the beginning. To be fair, this did produce one masterpiece of anticlimax –

'There was an old person of Anerly
Whose conduct was strange and unmannerly:
He rushed down the Strand
With a pig in each hand,
But returned in the evening to Anerly.'

I dread to think what kind of punchline the teams of 'I'm Sorry I Haven't A Clue' would have substituted for that.

HUMPH: We come to the game which is called 'Double Feature' and this starts from the premise that the international film industry is broke and that new films have to be remakes of old films.

BARRY: A conglomeration, Humph, they are combining the best elements of Nicholas and Alexandra and Bob and Carol and Ted and Alice and Pete and Tilli and calling it We Must Get a Larger Bed.

For many years of his life, my father kept a large, blue, hard-back notebook in which he wrote things which he read or heard that impressed, amused, moved or, sometimes, exasperated him. When he died, the book came into my possession briefly before I passed it to his nephew. There was little in the contents that would have surprised us. We have known since childhood that inside the eminent schoolmaster was a perpetual schoolboy, frequently let out, whose very un-commonplace enthusiasms often exceeded our own.

So we are not surprised by the seemingly random inclusion of the vital statistics of an elephant, in the light of a long-remembered visit to the annual Suffolk Show. He insisted that we should go with him expressly to see a Suffolk Punch cart-horse whose cause he had espoused, though he was by no stretch of the imagination a horseman. To us, one Suffolk Punch looked very much like another, but he fanned the embers of our expectation by assuring us that we would know the champion as soon as we saw him. And, sure enough, when the Naunton Prince did heave in sight, we had to acknowledge that, in the spring of his step and the magnificent arch of his neck, he was several cuts above the others.

A year later, when the muscle-bound champion collapsed and died, my father was much affected. Naunton Prince was rivalled in his affections only by Greta Garbo, at the climax of whose tragic movies he would reveal his emotion by standing up, clearing his throat noisily and putting on his rain coat.

A portait of Humph's father by the fire.

BUD FREEMAN.   CHICAGO.

"YEAH! BLOW THAT THING!"

This sketch, copied from photos, was found in a school scrapbook that was bought this year by Humph's sister, Mary, at auction. He has signed the drawings 'by kind permission'. He would have been about 14 years old at the time but had obviously learnt something about copyright!

A portrait of George Bernard Shaw that accompanied a provocative newspaper article written by the man of letters himself at the grand age of 93.

GREETINGS

From

XMAS 1954

Humph would always endeavour to make his own Christmas and birthday cards. Often these would be a mixture of calligraphy, cartoon and a liberal dose of cut and paste. The dogs – Brandy, Snuff (and later Whiskey) – played many a starring role!

"DAD SAYS 'E WOULDNT GIVE TUPPENCE FOR YOUR "SILENT NIGHT" BUT THERE'S TWO AND A TANNER WAITIN' FOR YER IF YOU COME AND BLOW UP THREE DOZEN BALLOONS "

It is an often made, yet understandable assumption that Dad imparted his love of the trumpet to his children. Not so! The reason for this is simple – he practised at home! Not only was it the tuneless screeching (apparently exercising his lips, rather than delivering a tune) but the sight of him emptying valves of spit was enough to put anyone off the whole idea.

*U*p early and straight up the M6 to Pebble Mill, to do the celebrity cookery spot in Pebble Mill at One. Have chosen the liver with basil recipe, which I gave over the phone last week to Mary Clyne, the cookery producer. She turned out to be a pleasant lady who took charge of me throughout. All the ingredients were laid out, and a finished product was all ready, congealing somewhat under the lights. Not much time for rehearsal since a team of Chinese musicians and dancers hogged all the rehearsal time. Turned out to be just as well, since everything went very fluently, with Donny McCleod prodding away at the liver as if he could hardly forbear to eat it! One thing – the basil looked odd, more like wood chips, and when I scattered them on, they turned everything orange! P.S. My name for the dish is Liver Prunella – after P. Scales, alias Sybil Fawlty. Why? 'Basull!!!'

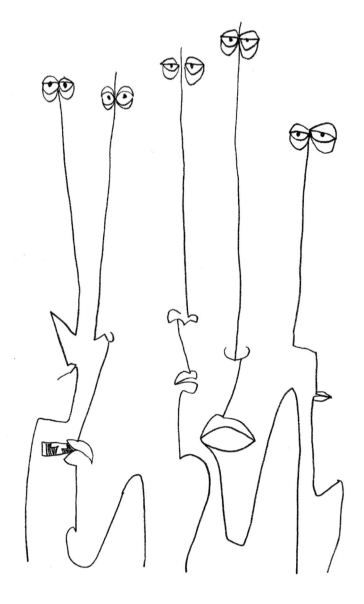

One of Humph's doodles that I found inside the cover of one of dad's many books on jazz.

For 10 years of our childhood, dad was writing restaurant reviews for Harpers and Queen. One of the obvious benefits was that we would eat out – a lot! In fact, we were often 'employed' by him to offer our critique of the food in front of us.

I have the Man-size Breakfast (what else?) with two eggs, two rashers of nice lean bacon and two firm, unwrinkled sausages, at 47p. My last visit was on the first new tax-day, and the waiter was enjoying it enormously. 'How the V.A.T. taste?' he asked at every table, 'is good?'

If you are strictly vegetarian, violently opposed to blood-sports and fanatical about the conservation of every living thing, it would perhaps be as well to give this a miss. I have always considered myself quite a mild person, but after an hour or two in the unashamedly predatory atmosphere of the large, smouldering-red room, I felt quite ferocious. Cases of impaled butterflies and stuffed birds, deers' heads, guns and less easily identifiable bits of lethal ironmongery festoon the walls.

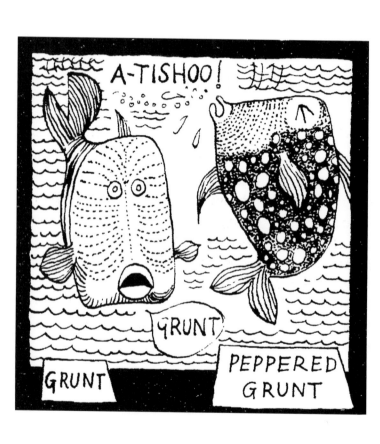

Tuesday 12th January 1983, Doha

Elsewhere there's a fine aquarium showing the local marine life. A glance at the catalogue suggests a pretty dangerous and unsavoury underworld below the waves. I wouldn't like to venture unaccompanied among the community of Snappers, Sweetlips, Scavengers, Silver Biddies, Porgies, Wrasses, Flutemouths, Clownfishes, Gobies, Blennies, Puffers, Triggerfishes and Grunts. (Travelling with a crew of itinerant musicians one encounters enough Peppered Grunts in the early morning without wanting to see them out under water!)

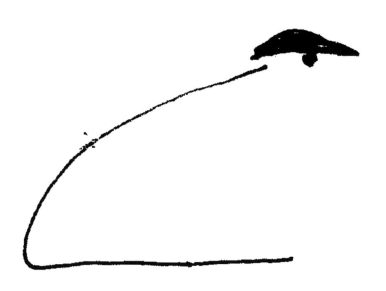

A cartoon of Ronnie Scott. Ronnie loved this doodle that Humph did on a scrap of paper. It was once considered for use on the club menu.

For a musician in the emerging jungle of jazz music in the 'twenties, however supreme his talent, survival meant being prepared at all times to do battle with predatory rivals. There are many tales of the formidable young Louis demolishing the opposition of men like Buddy Petit, Jabbo Smith and 'Hot Lips' Page. My own favourite was again provided by Lil Armstrong. She tells of a night in a Chicago club – in the mid-'twenties, I would guess – when Freddie Keppard, an established hero from New Orleans, tried to give Louis a lesson. After listening to Louis for a while, he said 'Boy, let me have that trumpet.' Then according to Lil, he 'blew and he blew and at the end the people gave him a nice hand. Then he handed the trumpet back to Louis and I said 'Get 'im! Get 'im!' Oooh! Never in my life did I hear such trumpet playing. If you want to hear Louis play, hear him when he's angry! Boy, he blew and people started standing up on tables and chairs. Screamin'. And Freddie, he just eased out!'

Freddy Keppard
eases out....

This is a satirical cartoon of George VI and his Queen (who later became fondly known as the Queen Mum). 'The King was in his counting house, counting all his money...'

The Ballet Dancer.

Some of Humph's earliest cartoons were found in the diary he wrote while working in the Port Talbot steel mills in 1940, aged 19. His early style is very distinctive.

A very curious figure in the lab: is a young coal-crusher who has the appearance of a Russian ballet dancer after an explosion. His waist is almost non-existent, and is hair is cut squarely all round. It would come as no surprise were he to suddenly leap onto the coal-slab and strike a pose, balanced on one toe.

Down among the jazzmen and the blues shouters, we find, naturally enough, a less timid and inhibited attitude to drink. Jazz was born in the honky-tonks and barrelhouses of New Orleans, where, for five cents a time, the customers helped themselves from the row of barrels along the wall. The repertoire of early jazz is full of titles with bibulous connections – 'In the Barrel', 'Gut-bucket Blues' (named after the bucket which caught the drippings or 'gutterings' from the barrels), 'Dead Drunk Blues', 'Moonshine Blues' and so on and so on.

immy Hastings, sax player in Humph's band (1993 to present day), used a circular breathing technique which enabled him to seemingly play a continuous solo for minutes without taking a breath. This doodle shows Humph had his own theories on how Jimmy achieved this.

We were all enrolled into in the RSPB's Young Ornithologist Club as soon as we could focus binoculars. Dad's passion for bird-watching was infectious. At times this would get the better of him and country drives became quite unpredictable, if not dangerous. He would often come to a sudden stop having spotted a shrike or suchlike in the hedgerows and, suffice to say, any cars following us were not best impressed.

Steve Voce is coming across to the session tonight and it is his birthday, so out of the remains of Dave Green's bird mags, and some fashion mags on the bedside table, I did him a montage of falcons, eyes and eyeless faces on the theme of Jack Sheldon's 'they love eyes'.

One of Humph's first cartoons to make the *Daily Mail* front page. The story it accompanies has a familiar ring – UK banks gambling on a rumour that the dollar may be devalued.

"Down one minute! – up the next! – I'm sick of all these rumours about the pound! Give me this lot in silver and coppers, please!"

*I*t's not generally known that I once, long ago, appeared in the radio series The Archers. *It was a bit of a let-down because I was expecting a day out at Ambridge, instead of which they recorded me in my back garden in Swiss Cottage – a small garden overlooked by houses.*

The BBC sound engineers set up a microphone in the middle of the lawn, and from there I was supposed to be the 'star' opening the Ambridge village fete. We did several takes because the producer kept telling me to shout louder. So there I stood in front of this solitary microphone in the middle of my lawn bellowing 'Ladies and Gentlemen…' at an imaginary crowd, while windows opened and heads appeared from every neighbouring house to see what this loony was doing.

Humphrey Lyttelton's own impression of the BBC task force that moved into his Hampstead flat to catch him and his family ' At Home ' last November

Stephane Grapelli told me that Django Reinhardt couldn't read or write, but he would always tag along with Stephane to business meetings which concerned the Hot Club of France. Apparently he would sit there pretending he could understand what was going on until he felt he ought to make his presence felt. At this point he would grab the contract from Stephane and point to a paragraph at random and say, 'Non, non.'

Invariably it would be the clause which said the band were guaranteed free accommodation and food.

Jack Teagarden   'Satchmo'   Django Reinhardt   Mezzmezzrow

HUMPHREY LYTTELTON
AND HIS BAND

Sunday
December 11th, 1955

Town Hall
Leeds

SOUVENIR PROGRAMME

PRICE ONE SHILLING

*T*he first band I ever sat in with was Carlo Krahmer's. At that time they were resident at the Nut House Club in Regent Street, where there used to be a fight every Saturday night with incidental music.

Variations
on a
theme...

This was drawn on one of the band's Middle East tours, Humph unites the countries visited in this detailed drawing of traditional head gear.

Wherever and whenever possible Humph would expound the virtues of good handwriting, signing up new members of the Society for Italic Handwriting along the way. One of his favourite stories of 'cacography' (bad handwriting) was that of Lady Colefax. The only hope of deciphering her invitations, someone said, was to pin them up on a wall and run past them! His father told of a note he received inviting him to dinner – 'We guessed that the time was 8 and not 3, as it appeared to be, but all we could tell about the day was that it was not Wednesday.'

Portrait of calligrapher Alfred Fairbank for the
Society of Italic Handwriting newsletter.

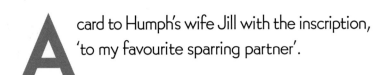

A card to Humph's wife Jill with the inscription, 'to my favourite sparring partner'.

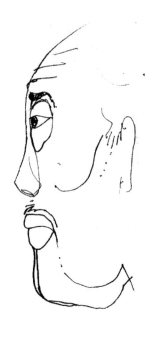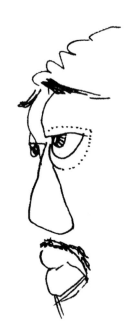

Once, in the late fifties, I was with Duke Ellington in his hotel suite when some London University students were interviewing him for their magazine. One of the more erudite among them asked Duke if he was offended when tenor sax player Jimmy Forrest borrowed a theme from his 'Happy-Go-Lucky Local' and had a huge hit with it under the title 'Night Train'.

Urbane as always, Duke said, 'No. It must be a good tune for so many people to want to write it.'

Bureaucracy can turn a mild-mannered citizen into a power-drunk overlord. The woman head of our local Food Office would have made an excellent drill sergeant for Hitler's legions.

Letter from 'Mailbag'

FORE!!!

Fettling for Victory

Billy Eckstine is a very keen golfer and he always plays when he's over here. One day, he was playing with the bassist Joe Muddel soon after Billy Daniels had been on tour here sporting a most indiscreet toupee. At one hole, Eckstine played a duff shot which dug up an enormous divot. He picked it up, put it on his head and started singing, 'That Old Black Magic...'.

*F*ormalities over, I am mingling when someone brings over a distinguished-looking grey-haired man and introduces him as Mr So-and-so (a Turkish-sounding name), the Jordanian Director of Planning and Foreign Relations at the Department of Health. Without preamble he whips a mouth-organ out of the top pocket of his dinner-jacket and launches into 'I Got Rhythm', staring at me intently over his cupped hands. He plays quite well in a sort of Larry Adler fashion, but there's nothing more embarrassing than being played at, eyeball to eyeball, and I'm glad when he stops.

Port Talbot, 1940

Another incident, which might have ended in tears, occurred as we were leaving lunch one day. We have to pass out over the level crossing, where there is usually a policeman on guard. This time was no exception and as we came up he did an unexpected thing and demanded to see our passes and identity cards. Normally, now that our faces are known, we walk in without any bother, and this sudden demand as we were going out took me quite unawares. I could find neither of my cards!! Frantically, I fumbled through every pocket, already seeing visions of firing squads and prison squares. The policeman merely stood with hand outstretched, and gazed casually round as though he had known all along that I was a spy. At last! my fingers, trembling 'like aspirin leaves', closed upon the truant pass, and I was allowed to pedal off, leaving the policeman shaking his head disconsolately, his hopes of promotion shattered.

This is a cartoon that accompanied an article on Lawrence Wright. Wright put on the annual production 'On With the Show' at Blackpool for 32 years. He was presented with an Ivor Novello Award in 1962 for 'outstanding service to British popular and light music'. He also established *The Melody Maker* magazine in 1926.

humph

A jolly day. Jill, Nana and I went to a drinks party with Liz and Howard in Hadley Road. About 20 people, mostly neighbours of theirs and a few people from Howard's firm. Discovered from a Nigerian that several of the Arabic phrases I learnt are the same in Nigeria, but pronounced differently. Ali and Stephen were there. We met Liz's mum, who has moved down to Barnet from her home near Morpeth in Northumbria. Georgie's geography teacher Rita was there, too – we asked her to our party next Sunday. Liz said that they were going to a carol service at the church near Hadley Green gate, so we agreed to meet them there.

Nice little church, small and either modern or newly refurbished – and warm, thank goodness! We were shown to the overflow seats behind the organist, which provided entertainment in itself. Halfway through 'God rest ye merry...' his innumerable little bits of music fell off the rack, leaving him floundering. The beaming Black man who took the collection turned out to be General Gowon, former ruler of Nigeria.

At the sound of a lone clarinet,
I shouted 'Stand back, I'm a vet!'
Picture Acker's alarm
As I thrust in my arm.
Oh God, I still drink to forget!

I suppose you think you know all there is to know about limericks. That turns out on investigation to be precious little – and negative at that. For starters, the title has nothing to do with the Irish town of Limerick. True, word has been put about in the past that it derives from the chorus 'Will you come up to Limerick?' sung between impromptu and naughty verses composed at convivial parties. But to date, no one has ever been found to admit to singing such verses. Would you? Well then...

Even more far-fetched is the theory that the ribald verse-form was brought back to Limerick by veterans of the Irish Brigade in 1791 who had served in France for a hundred years. The evidence?

'Digerie, Digerie, Doge
La souris ascend l'horloge...'

Stop right there! Translated into English (presumably to avoid having to find a rhyme for 'horloge') that's 'Hickory, Dickery, Dock' – and any child of five knows that's not a limerick. It's not nearly filthy enough.

Monday 24th June 1974

Wimbledon starts today on television – a change from World Cup football, from which Scotland were absquatulated by Yugoslavia on Saturday. I dislike tennis – both the game and those who play it. The women especially are a horrific lot, talking in terms of 'possessing' their opponents when on court. Commentator Maurice Eddlestone, who is given to overt romanticising, came up with one of his gems of waffle. After a player won a point to draw level, he said, 'Well, that's this game of tennis – one moment you're ahead, then you're level, next minute you're behind, then you're level again.'

you can't wear
the same
hat all the
time...

Thelonious Monk

*T*helonious Monk was everyone's idea of the taciturn modern jazz musician – dark glasses, goatee beard and all. We toured in America in 1959 on a coach that had my band and the Monk Quartet on board. Monk sat on the coach day after day totally silent. Then one day, a dog or something ran across the road, the driver hit the brakes and all the baggage fell off the racks. Monk stood up, said, 'Well, shut my mouth wide open,' sat down and never spoke another word for the rest of the tour.

The hat had been given to him by an admirer. It was a sort of wickerwork lampshade, or inverted fruit basket, probably Chinese in origin, with long straps which dangled over the ears. We got to know that hat well since at no time in the day (or, presumably, night) did Monk remove it. For ten days it was a fixture. Then on the eleventh day, boarding the coach in Boston, Massachusetts, Monk appeared in a different hat. It was a grey, bulbous affair which mystified us until we recognized it as a homburg in the state in which it was stored on the hatter's shelf, before a gentle karate chop had given it the conventional dent in the top. 'Hey, Monk, you've changed your hat!' someone cried in amazement. 'Sure,' said Monk without a flicker, 'you can't wear the same hat all the time.'

Here are a few autobiographical drawings ...and Humph's own words.

In every other respect I was a model art student.

I was encouraged to regard myself as an established cartoonist.

It is popular Jazz which 'classical' music lovers mean when they talk about 'that dreadful jazz!'

The clientele was a mixed one. There were plenty of GI's, quite a number of guards...

I wanted to play, and that in its turn fostered an ambition, almost sub-conscious at first, to lead a band of my own.

Dad's penchant for cartooning and doodling was taken to the extreme with his piano. We never found out the history behind this one but during one of the many jazz parties held at his Belsize Park flat probably had something to do with it!

When Graeme Bell and his band were over here in 1951 they got a booking in a hall called Barrowland in Glasgow. It was one of those places where, when the curtain goes up, you find a line of bouncers, arms linked, facing the audience. Well, everybody in London was telling them to be careful up there in Glasgow.

It is no secret that Australians are quite fond of a bit of aggro, so they set off in their coach and fists were clenched before they reached Watford. As it turned out, the first half was very quiet, just the odd crash of breaking glass, but basically they were ignored as nobody was interested.

During the second half, however, Graeme was playing away at the piano when out of the corner of his eye he saw a figure climb on to the stage and advance towards him. On the principle of 'Don't shoot until you see the whites of their eyes', he went on playing until the figure was right at his shoulder – then in one movement he turned round and let fly. An autograph book went one way, a pen the other. He'd laid out the only fan they had in the place.

Actually, people think I am not much of a sportsman, but when I was at Eton I was a deadly fast bowler. In fact one day, when I was running up to bowl, the ball flew out of the back of my hand and hit the old man who used to walk around the boundary selling sweets. It broke his knee.

First impression of Trevor.

(Second impression (more accurate) of Mr Trevor).

Humph's Port Talbot diaries document important friendships which played a significant role in his changing political and social outlook. However, in this instance, he obviously failed to see past Mr. Trevor's features.

W e met a new character today, not quite so attractive as our former acquaintances. He is Mr. Trevor (I don't know whether this is his Christian or surname) and he is in charge of the washing and 'rectification'. Pleasant to talk to, he has, however, a very unattractive appearance – hunch-backed, pigeon-toed, with flapping ears and a toothless grin, he is like a very decrepit cross between a rodent and a chimpanzee.

We have arrived at the conclusion that we simply cannot bear the sight of Mr. Trevor – he's altogether too noisy and hideous. He smokes all day long, clutching his cigarette as a gorilla holds a banana; and, worst of all, he's had his hair cut down to a grey stubble, like the back of a mangy rat.

The more general objection to the juggling of tapes after a session is finished is that it makes for artificial perfection at the expense of realism. The record purchaser feels that he is not getting the real thing – that the music he hears on his record is not what came out at the time, but is the result of manipulation afterwards. But is any record realistic? There are shortcomings in the actual process of recording which make a certain amount of faking necessary. When the clarinettist stands nearer to the microphone than the trumpeter, to achieve the effect of lifelike balance, he is making a concession to artificiality.

*J*ohn Picard played trombone with my band for nearly ten years. At first he played a sort of rugged Dixieland style. Later he passed through mainstream jazz on to the avant garde, a fact which I discovered to my cost recently.

Promoters are always asking me to 'recreate' my earlier bands and we did one concert in Weston-super-Mare in which I had John Picard, Wally Fawkes and Kathy Stobart as guests, to represent my bands from the 1950s and 1960s.

At Sunday concerts in Weston-super-Mare the front three rows are taken up by elderly ladies of frail disposition. When John came on for his set, he immediately switched into his avant-garde mode. When it came to his first solo he got so close to the microphone that it was actually inside the bell of the trombone, and unleashed a stentorian bellow which must have shunted most of the front row straight into intensive care.

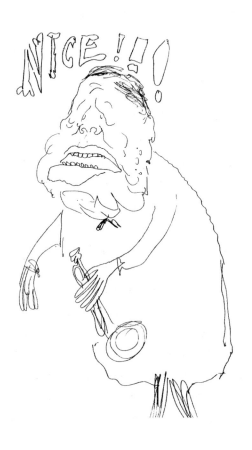

The immortal New Orleans jazz trumpeter, Henry 'Red' Allen, caricatured on a scrap of paper. Like Humph, his career spanned six decades. Humph was a great fan of Red and had championed his trumpet playing for many years.

However, they once briefly fell out during a session over what turned out to be a minor misunderstanding. It became obvious something was wrong when Red started interrupting the piano solos by calling in another soloist. It turned out that Red had misunderstood a band catch phrase – 'moving on up' – that had been called out by Joe Temperley just as Red was giving the audience his renowned verbal jazz history. He wrongly assumed that they were in some way hinting to him that he was dwelling in the past. Red, momentarily losing his temper, started to harangue the band over the microphone, stating, 'I can move up on you guys anytime.'

To cut a long story short, the feud continued for a while but the two trumpeters were soon reconciled with each other and Humph took Red out for a Chinese meal.

*I*f you were to slice the audience at a popular jazz concert clean down the middle, you would find an almost complete cross-section of the nation. Within this cross-section there are any number of distinctions and shades of taste and behaviour, and it is when you start to analyse these that the fun really starts. Why is it that the 'eggheads' – intellectuals, university students and so on – favour the simple structures and basic rhythms of 'traditional' jazz while those at the Teddy Boy end of the social scale go for the more cerebral 'modern' jazz? Several of our Angry Young Men – Kingsley Amis, John Wain, Kenneth Tynan – are acknowledged jazz fans, sometimes dabbling in a little part-time criticism. Oddly enough, they tend to identify themselves with past eras – the twenties, the Chicago epoch, Jelly Roll Morton, Bix Beiderbecke – and to cold-shoulder the angry and disillusioned young men of modern jazz. No doubt there are good psychological reasons for this paradox.

Intellectuals favour the simple structure of traditional jazz

Next, please! Political talk bores me – and as the world's champion talkers are British barbers I shall do without a haircut until after the election.

Letter from 'Mailbag'

humph

Port Talbot, 1940

The rest of Saturday was spent in cinema and lodging. The films were good this week, even though every programme is marred by that intolerable bounder R.E. Jeffrey, and by the 'Cowshed Clappers'. By the way, Frank's little parting joke in the morning was to stick a card saying 'For sale, cash only, no dealers, sold in parts,' onto our bikes. At first, we did not know who had done it, but when Frank emerged from his hut shaking with silent laughter we knew at once. (Another of our discoveries has been that Frank is the father of Hayden Roberts – fancy that shy, frail little clerk being the son of the substantial Frank. 'Mrs Roberts must be very intelligent' is the only conclusion which can be drawn.)

For most of our childhood we had three dogs. I wouldn't say dad was a dog lover, more a dog tolerator. When my mother decided to get a cat (13 eventually) I had left home. However, there was many a despairing phone call: 'We've got another bloody cat'. His main objection was having to rescue mutilated birds outside his study window.

In 1984, near the start of my record label, Calligraph, I asked the late Ted Taylor if, for convenience, he knew of a good photographer near his studio in Kent, where we recorded. He said, 'There's one just up the road – I'll get her to pop by next time you're here.' Rosie popped by, and has been with us ever since. Why? In a sentence, photographers who move in on a bunch of musicians, control them like a benevolent drill-sergeant, have a laugh, come up with great ideas, get the job done in minimum time and with maximum results – well, they don't pop by every day of the week. Rosie's not just a photographer, she's on the family!

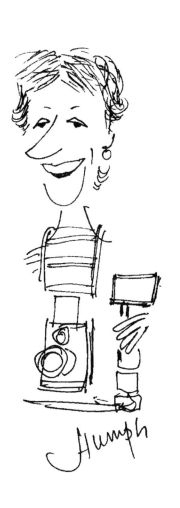

"...HAD A LETTER FROM HIM THIS MORNING."

Humph's cartoon of Sinclair Traill, editor of *Jazz Journal* from 1947 to 1982.

Sinclair was a great name-dropper and, if a name came up in conversation – Louis Armstrong or Duke Ellington – Sinclair would stroke his moustache and say, 'That's funny, I had a letter from him this morning.'

Humph knew this. For some reason Sarah Vaughan had written to Humph and he carried that letter round in his inside pocket waiting to meet Sinclair. They met at a dinner party and Humph contrived to bring the conversation round to the subject of Sarah Vaughan.

'That's funny,' said Sinclair. 'I had a letter from her this morning.'

'So did I!', shouted Humph in triumph, dragging the letter from his pocket.

Steve Voce

HUMPH: We go on now to the game 'Word for Word' and in this round one of the members of the team says a word and his partner must say another word totally unconnected with the first, and so on.

WILLY: Pump.

TIM: Gerbil.

WILLY: Bottle.

HUMPH: I have a challenge there from Barry.

BARRY: Making a gerbil in a bottle is a very old pastime. It replaced ships years ago.

WILLY: I knew there was a connection.

HUMPH: I've got one on my mantelpiece.

*D*iscography, like philately, is a complex study. The professional discographer has to combine the qualities of a statistician, musicologist and sleuth.

Everybody waitin' for Bean to talk....

Coleman Hawkins

I once did the shortest interview in history with Coleman Hawkins. A BBC producer thought it would be a great idea for me to interview some jazz stars at the Philharmonic backstage before a concert. So I had to go into the communal dressing-room, with camera man and sound recorder in tow, just as they were getting ready to go on. Eventually I reached Coleman Hawkins, who had been glowering at me from the corner. I said, 'I believe you know a good friend of mine,' and named the person. He said, 'Nope,' and that was it. End of interview.

humph

The 'Daily Mailbag' of 1949 was not short of letters regarding ladies' fashion. Humph drew this column breaker in response to a reader's observation that the dictates of ladies fashion became more absurd and expensive every day. He (or she) goes on to suggest that, until the financial crisis had passed, fashions should be nationalised and designs 'frozen' on the simplest lines! Take note, Gordon Brown!

This 1949 cartoon accompanied 'The Daily Mail End of the Year Quiz' on the eve of a new decade.

Port Talbot, 1940

Lunch at the canteen has been, as usual, very entertaining. Bowen told a story the other day which reduced everyone to helpless giggles. He took a pair of trousers to be altered, and the old tailor looked at them and scratched his head. 'No!' he muttered, 'I can't see what's wrong with them.' Suddenly his face lit up, 'Ay! I've got it!' he cried, 'Those trousers 'ave got two left legs!!' Mr B. then went to Burfoots to be fitted for an overcoat. 'Do you want to measure me?' he asked. 'No,' they said, 'We'll take measurements from your coat.' 'But,' argued Bowen, 'You can't put a thing inside a thing that's the same size as the first thing!' In spite of this overwhelming logic, the tailors were persistent. So now, when Mr Bowen wants to put on his overcoat he has to take his jacket off!!

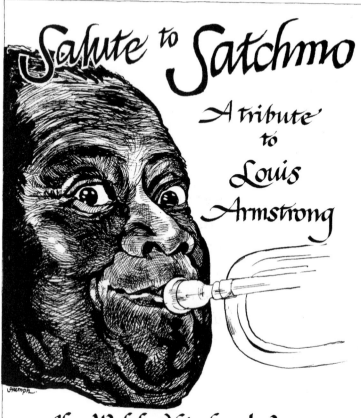

Salute to Satchmo

A tribute to Louis Armstrong

Alex Welsh & his band & guests
Humphrey Lyttelton
George Chisholm - Bruce Turner

SOUVENIR PROGRAMME

In jazz, it has been quite usual for musicians under contract to one record company to record for another anonymously.

Early in his career, Louis Armstrong was caught out. His recording boss recognised his playing and confronted him. Louis said, 'That's not me...but I won't do it again.'

The late Pete Strange, trombonist in Humph's band for 21 years, was an extremely easy-going and placid character. Humph drew this on the occasion of Pete 'losing it' in a rare expression of anger.

Mr Hyde

The Porthcawl club. House!

Port Talbot, 1940

We set out on bicycles to the Pyle and Kenfig golf course, to spend a pleasant afternoon free from the revolting odours in which we spent the last week. We got there eventually, to find a very smart club-house, complete with the full regiment of staring imbeciles without which no club-house can rightly claim to be a club-house. They stared solidly as we went in, stared solidly as we came out; fat overdressed men and fat overpainted women with legs like those found on the bulkier type of Bechstein grand, and eyes like unsympathetic prawns.

Humph was an avid sunworshipper and would expose his substantial frame to the 'rays' whenever possible. On holiday in Italy precautions were taken to cover sensitive areas from the unforgiving sun. Unfortunately a single big toe was left exposed to the elements. To the obvious amusement of his children, Humph could only wear one sandal for some days.

A very early cartoon unearthed by Humph's daughter, Henrietta. I can imagine Humph's reaction if asked what this depicted... 'Gawd knows!' Suggestions on a postcard please.

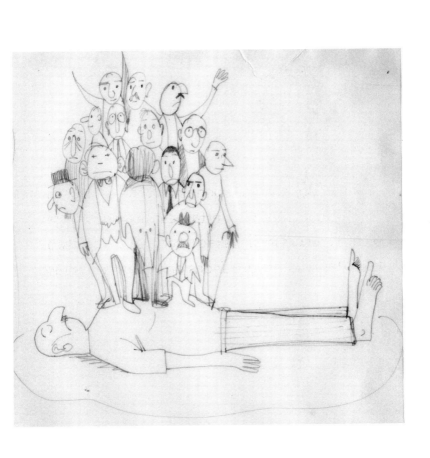

During the recording of 'Trouble in Mind' at our home studio, Humph spotted the bongos. A wedding gift to our eldest son and wife, the bongos were sitting pretty and unused. Humph spontaneously started tapping away on them. Being the first person to play them, we asked him if he could leave his mark on the skins. He graciously gratified us and within moments he had adorned both skins with two self portraits.

Not long after, we were trying to come up with a logo for our record company, Slave To The Rhythm Records, which produced 'Trouble in Mind'. We requested permission from Humph to use his 'Humph the Bongo King' as our company logo, as it shows him slaving to the rhythm. We couldn't have come up with anything more fitting than that.

Elkie Brookes

*B*en Webster was once escorted down the stairs by two young policemen after an unruly session at the Dancing Slipper Club in Nottingham. Halfway down, he turned to one of them and asked, 'Did you know Art Tatum?'

Ben Webster

'**H**umph at the Conway' was an album I made back in 1954, and it had just been re-released with the original cover design and sleeve note which refers to our playing a concert every month in the Conway Hall in London.

In 1991 I received a letter from a young man saying that he had bought the record and this was just the sort of jazz concert he would like to visit, so could I tell him when the next one was. He went on to point out that he'd passed the Conway Hall recently and that I ought to know that there were no posters outside publicising our concerts.

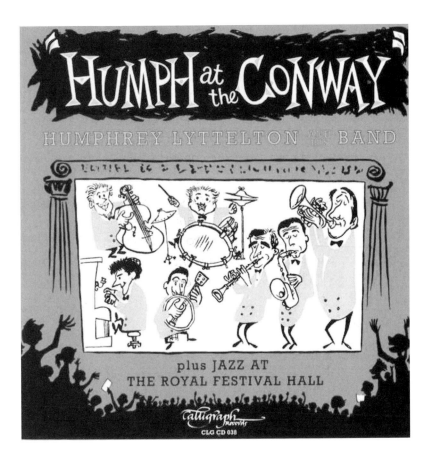

Modern jazz musicians have grown into a species clearly distinguishable from the traditionalist

Modern jazz musicians are more closely associated with their idols across the Atlantic, and, through imitation, have grown into a species clearly distinguishable from the traditionalist. There's little 'artiness' among the modernists. Instead of the beards, the vivid shirts and the sandals, they exhibit their up-to-dateness with crew cuts, streamlined American-style suiting, and sundry affectations – rimless glasses, dark glasses, lapel-free jackets, and so on – of contemporary transatlantic origin.

*A*t one time we used to sing the 'Whiffenpoof Song', with me, Tony Coe and Joe Temperley singing close harmony around one microphone. Unfortunately, Joe and Tony were heavily into Indian food at the time and after about forty bars I began to lapse into unconsciousness.

The Whiffenpoof Song—
curned style

Monday 13th October 1980

Gig at Tonbridge School. Left at about 4.30 to drive down. Reception in the headmaster's office beforehand, met one 'contemporary at Eton', one 'second cousin by marriage', one 'old friend from Sandhurst'. The latter conducted a conversation by repeating one's answers to his questions. 'Do you travel much?' 'Quite a bit.' 'Ah, quite a bit...yes...yes.' Concert was very successful and the band played well.

'It has occurred to me, gentlemen, that while the pressing affairs of state hamper our artistic activities, we should at least endeavour to achieve a high standard of doodling.'

Port Talbort, 1940

Our studies were interrupted by a siren to which we paid little heed; we remained in the office, and watched the men running like ants over the buildings and down to the shelters where they stood, scanning the sky. As old Blacklegs said yesterday, if they don't go into the shelter, they might just as well stay at work.

SHELTER

Study of Welsh workmen taking cover

SIDE ONE NOW THAT WE'RE HERE, LET'S GO! ○ ECHOES OF HARLEM ○

CARIBANA QUEEN ○

ROBIN'S NEST ○ HARBOURFRONT RAGTIME ○ MISS MATILDA ○

THREE LITTLE WORDS ○

TOOT SWEET ○

HUMPH at the BULL'S HEAD

HUMPHREY LYTTELTON & HIS BAND 'LIVE', NOV. 15, 1984

Calligraph Records

○ HIGH SOCIETY ○ DO NOTHING TILL YOU HEAR FROM ME ○ SIDE TWO ○

Another of Humph's album sleeves. This one was for a live album recorded at one of his favourite venues, the Bull's Head in Barnes.

*S*ession at the Bull's Head. Arrived to find Mick P. fiddling with the P.A. Halfway thru' the first chorus I had it switched off. By challenging the audience to keep quiet ('we won't deafen you with amplification – so don't deafen us!') I got reasonable quiet and we had a fine session.

I discovered this doodle on the back of one of the envelopes in which his script for our tour show in Buxton was contained. It would have been done on Monday 10th March 2009, as that was the date of the show. I seldom discovered doodles on Humph's 'Clue' scripts or their envelopes, presumably as there wasn't much spare time for him to complete them.

Jon Naismith,
Producer of *I'm Sorry I Haven't A Clue*

As President of The Society for Italic Handwriting my father was always keen on finding converts to the cause. I am happy to have been one of them.

*H*aving met on my tours many people who have an interest in nice-looking handwriting but know nothing of our existence, I have a good idea of the thought that enters some minds when they are presented with the news that there is a Society for Italic Handwriting. 'Ah yes, another arty-crafty bring-back-the-Spinning-Jenny bunch of cranks. They'd have us using quills next – AND drying the ink with sand, I shouldn't wonder!'

I must confess that similar thoughts entered my mind when, in the early Fifties, my father began receiving the Bulletins of this Society. Then, finding them lying about on his desk amid letters from fellow enthusiasts, I began to read on. There were also articles and letters – full of enthusiasm and humour – which addressed themselves to the everyday and still-relevant problems of how to write legibly and with a style which gives pleasure to reader and writer alike. Here was a society of italic handwriters, many of whom had contrived to convert an ill-taught hand resembling a tangled string into something handsome and artistic. This is the society of which I am proud to be President.

TAILPIECE. . .

BY

Humphrey Lyttelton